Fact Finders®

INVENT IT

# BUILD IT

### INVENT NEW STRUCTURES AND CONTRAPTIONS

by Tammy Enz

**Project Consultant**
Daniel Enz, P.E. PhD
Assistant Professor, General Engineering
University of Wisconsin, Platteville

CAPSTONE PRESS
a capstone imprint

Fact Finders are published by Capstone Press,
1710 Roe Crest Drive, North Mankato, Minnesota 56003
www.capstonepub.com

 Books published by Capstone Press are manufactured with paper
containing at least 10 percent post-consumer waste.

*Library of Congress Cataloging-in-Publication Data*
Enz, Tammy.
  Build it : invent new structures and contraptions / by Tammy Enz.
      p. cm.—(Fact finders. Invent it)
  Includes bibliographical references and index.
  Summary: "Explains the principles of inventing and provides photo-illustrated instructions for making
a variety of structures and contraptions"—Provided by publisher.
  ISBN 978-1-4296-7635-9 (library binding)
  ISBN 978-1-4296-7981-7 (paperback)
  1. Structural engineering—Experiments—Juvenile literature.  I. Title. II. Series.
  TA634.E59 2012
  621—dc23                                                          2011028736

**Editorial Credits**
Christopher L. Harbo, editor; Sarah Bennett, designer; Eric Gohl, media researcher; Marcy Morin,
    scheduler; Sarah Schuette, photo stylist; Laura Manthe, production specialist

**Photo Credits**
Capstone Studio/Karon Dubke, all cover and interior project photos
Shutterstock: Alsu, 27 (bottom), ampFotoStudio, 8 (bottom), Lsaloni, 13, Qeen, 19

**Design Elements**
Shutterstock: alekup, liskus, Sylverarts, Tropinina Olga

Printed in the United States of America in Brainerd, Minnesota.
102011      006406BANGS12

# CONTENTS

# BUILDING SOLUTIONS

The world is full of wonderful, puzzling, everyday problems waiting to be solved. Inventing contraptions to solve those problems is what engineers do. But you don't need to be an engineer to invent like one. Just look at the problems around you. Ask how you can solve them. Tinker with things you find laying around the house. Try using them in new ways to solve the problems. Be creative. The crazier your ideas, the more fun you will have. It's time to start exploring your engineering genius.

## THE SIX STEPS OF INVENTING

Engineers and inventors follow a certain method when inventing. This method helps them build on their successes and learn from their failures. Inventors call the method's steps by different names, but the basics are always the same. Follow these six steps to see how inventing works:

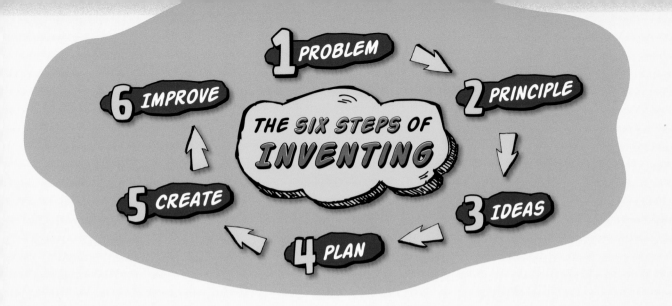

**1 PROBLEM** Inventors usually start with a problem. Ask yourself—What problem am I trying to solve?

**2 PRINCIPLE** Principles are basic rules or laws for how things work. Gravity is a principle that explains why a ball falls when you drop it. Friction is a principle that slows a ball down when you roll it across the floor. Ask yourself—What rules or laws apply to the problem I'm trying to solve?

**3 IDEAS** Write down some ideas that could help solve your problem. Be creative. Then pick the idea you think will work the best.

**4 PLAN** Plan how to build your device. Gather the tools and supplies needed.

**5 CREATE** Put everything together, and make something new.

**6 IMPROVE** Once the solution is created, ask yourself if it solved the problem. If not, what can you change? If so, how can you make it better?

For each invention you build, the process starts all over again. Let's see these six steps in action with the inventions in this book.

# DOOR PULLEY

**1 PROBLEM** Getting out of bed to open or close your bedroom door is a real pain. How can you build something that will open and close the door from across the room?

**2 PRINCIPLE** Opening and closing a door requires pulling and pushing **forces**. Can you use these forces to open and close a door from a distance?

**3 IDEAS** Pulling a door toward you is easy. You just tie a string to the knob. But how can a string push the door away from you? **Pulleys** are simple machines that use strings to lift and lower objects. Could you use a pulley system to pull the door open and closed?

**4 PLAN**

Gather together:
- ✔ masking tape
- ✔ scissors
- ✔ string
- ✔ adhesive wall hook
- ✔ 2 metal soup can rings

**force**—any action that changes the movement of an object
**pulley**—a grooved wheel turned by a rope, belt, or chain that often moves heavy objects

**1** Tape the door latch flat so it doesn't catch.

**2** Use a scissors to cut one piece of string about 8 feet (2.4 meters) long. Tie one end of the string to the knob on the inside of your room.

**3** Cut a second piece of string about 12 feet (3.7 m) long. Tie one end of this string to the knob on the outside of the door.

**4** Find a spot on the wall opposite the outside doorknob. Attach the adhesive wall hook to this spot.

**5** Run the long string through the hook. Then thread the rest of the string through the crack at the back of the door.

CONTINUED ON NEXT PAGE ➡

**6** Tie one ring to the end of each string for handles.

**7** Pull one string. Then pull the other. This action will open and close the door.

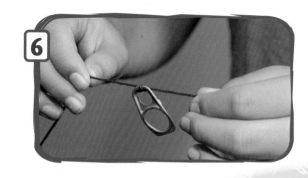

### 6 IMPROVE

Does your invention work? Experiment with the location of the hook. You might have to put it up high so people can walk under the string. Try using fishing line instead of string to make the door pulley invisible.

## ➡ SUCCESS FROM FAILURE

Not all new inventions turn out the way people expect. In 1894 John and Will Kellogg set out to invent a new kind of whole grain bread. While boiling wheat for the experiment, they were suddenly called away. They returned days later to find a soggy over-cooked mess. They rolled out the wheat and let it dry anyway. But the wheat grains turned into flakes instead of bread dough. Instead of bread, the brothers had invented cereal flakes. The Kelloggs' failure led to the invention of corn flakes cereal!

# NEWSPAPER FORT

## 1 PROBLEM

Newspapers pile up day after day. There must be something fun to do with them. Could newspapers be used to build a fort?

## 2 PRINCIPLE

Large buildings use **trusses** to support their heavy roofs. These frameworks use thin members, such as beams, to span great distances. Can you use truss action to make a newspaper fort?

## 3 IDEAS

Trusses are used to build towers, tunnels, and domes.

The key is that the members of a truss meet only at their ends and form a triangular shape. Newspaper can be rolled to make truss members. Can you connect rolled newspapers in a way that uses the triangular shape of truss action?

## 4 PLAN

Gather together:
- ✔ 195 full sheets of newspaper
- ✔ masking tape
- ✔ marker
- ✔ yardstick
- ✔ scissors
- ✔ stapler and staples

**truss**—a wooden or metal framework used to support walls or a roof

CONTINUED ON NEXT PAGE ➔

9

## **5 CREATE**

**1** Stack three sheets of newspaper. Starting at one corner, roll the papers tightly into a tube. Tape the tube to keep it from unrolling. Repeat this step until you have 65 tubes.

**2** Use a marker and a yardstick to mark the center of one newspaper roll. Measure and mark 14 inches (36 centimeters) on each side of the center mark. Use the scissors to cut the tube at these marks.

**3** Using this tube as a pattern, cut off the ends of 34 more newspaper rolls. Use a marker to label each of these tubes with a letter A.

**4** Find and mark the center of one of the remaining rolls. Measure and mark 13 inches (33 cm) on each side of this mark. Use the scissors to cut the tube at these marks.

**5** Using this tube as a pattern, cut off the ends of the remaining 29 newspaper rolls. Label each of these tubes with a letter B.

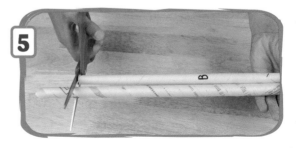

**6** Make a circle with 10 A tubes. Staple their ends together.

**7** Staple two A tubes into a V shape. Then staple the open ends of this A-tube V to two joints in the circle from step 6.

**8** Staple two B tubes into a V shape. Then staple the open ends of this B-tube V to two joints in the circle. Note how the B-tube V follows the A-tube V and shares one of its joints.

**9** Make four more V shapes with A tubes. Then make four more V shapes with B tubes. Staple them to the joints in the circle in the same alternating pattern. Each A-tube V should follow a B-tube V.

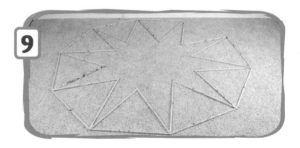

**10** Staple 10 B tubes to the top points of the Vs to connect them. The first row of the dome is complete.

CONTINUED ON NEXT PAGE ➡

**11** Staple one B tube to the top point of each B-tube V in the first row. These five B tubes should point toward the center of the circle.

**12** Staple two A tubes to the end of each B tube added in step 11. Angle these tubes back toward the first row. Staple the free ends to the top points of the A-tube Vs in the first row.

**13** Staple five A tubes to the points near the top of the dome to connect them. The second row of the dome is complete.

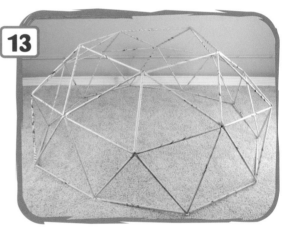

**14** Staple the last five B tubes to the joints in the second row. Each tube will meet at the top of the dome. Staple the tubes where they meet to complete the dome.

## 6 IMPROVE

Does your newspaper fort support itself? Once you understand truss action, you can use it for all types of structures. Can you make a tower? A tunnel? What else can you make with trusses?

### ➡ UNCANNY INVENTION

In 1810 Peter Durand invented something everyone wanted and needed. His tin can for storing and preserving food saved many from starvation. But getting the cans open was a real battle. People used chisels and hammers to hack the cans open. People waited almost 50 years before Ezra Warner invented and **patented** a can opener in 1858. Imagine how many injuries opening cans caused before that invention!

**patent**—a legal document giving an inventor sole rights to make and sell an item he or she invented

# TRASH GRABBER

TRASH GRABBER

**1 PROBLEM** Garbage clutters parks, streets, and lawns. What kind of device would be most helpful to pick up the trash?

**2 PRINCIPLE** A device that grabs trash needs to open and close. A hinge is a simple machine that opens and closes. Can you use hinge action to grab objects?

**3 IDEAS** Hinges are most common on doors. Wire can make a simple hinge too. It can bend and spring back in place as long as it is not bent too far.

**4 PLAN**

Gather together:
- ✔ 4 4-foot (1.2 m) long pieces of 16-gauge galvanized wire
- ✔ masking tape
- ✔ 32-inch long (81-cm) piece of ½ inch (1.3 cm) PVC pipe
- ✔ soup can

hinge—a movable joint

14

**1** Bundle all four wires together lengthwise. Make sure the ends are even. Starting at one end, wind tape around the wires to hold them together. Continue winding for 3 feet (0.9 m).

**2** Insert the taped end of the wire bundle into one end of the pipe.

**3** Extend the taped end about 6 inches (15 cm) out of the pipe. Bend this portion into a hook for a handle.

**4** On the other end of the pipe, shape the bare end of each wire around the soup can. Each wire should form a hooked "claw" that bends inward.

**5** Slowly pull up the handle of the device to close the hooks around a piece of trash. Push down the handle to open the hooks and release the trash.

## 6 IMPROVE

Does your trash grabber work? Can you improve it to pick up smaller pieces of trash? Are there other ways to make a hinge? Could you use a door hinge with a pulley system to open and close a grabbing device?

# COIN SORTER

**1 PROBLEM** Spare change has a way of collecting in wallets, purses, and odd containers. What kind of machine could help sort your mixed coins?

**2 PRINCIPLE** Many engineering problems involve coming up with ways to sort objects. This principle is called **classification**. Objects can be classified by shape, weight, or size.

**3 IDEAS** Since coins are the same shape, can you think of ways to classify them by weight or by size? Can you make a device that allows heavier coins to fall in different places? Or can you come up with a way to let coins drop through different size holes?

**4 PLAN**

Gather together:
- ✔ shoe box
- ✔ ruler
- ✔ scissors
- ✔ cardboard
- ✔ pencil
- ✔ coins
- ✔ utility knife
- ✔ sandpaper
- ✔ hot glue gun and glue
- ✔ ribbon or string

**classification**—separating objects into groups by size, shape, or weight

**5 CREATE**

**1** Measure the shoe box's width and depth with a ruler. Use a scissors to cut three pieces of cardboard to match the measurements you made.

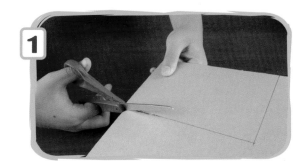

**2** Trace a nickel in the center of one piece of cardboard with a pencil. Have an adult help you carefully cut out the circle with a utility knife. Use sandpaper to smooth the edges of the hole so a nickel can slide through it.

**3** Repeat step 2 on the other two pieces of cardboard. Use a penny on one piece. Use a dime on the other piece.

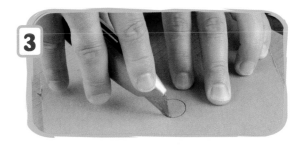

**4** Set the box on one end. Slide the cardboard with the nickel-sized hole into the box. Hot glue it in place about one quarter of the distance from the top end of the box.

**5** Slide the cardboard with the penny-sized hole into the center of the box. Hot glue it in place.

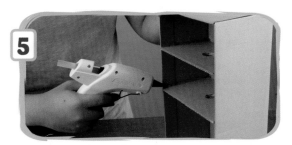

CONTINUED ON NEXT PAGE →

**6** Slide the cardboard with the dime-sized hole into the box. Hot glue it in place about one quarter of the distance from the bottom end of the box.

**7** With an adult's help, cut a small trapdoor on the top end of the box with the utility knife. Glue a loop of ribbon to the underside of the trapdoor. Close the flap, leaving the ribbon sticking out. Use the ribbon to open the flap.

**8** Place the lid on the box. Pour a handful of mixed coins into the trapdoor. Hold the lid in place as you shake the box for a minute or two.

**9** Open the box to see if the coins sorted into quarters, nickels, pennies, and dimes.

Did your coin sorter work? Would it work better with more holes on each shelf? Can you invent a machine that separates coins by weight?

## ➡ PATIENCE PAYS OFF

Sometimes people invent things no one needs—yet. Garrett Morgan patented a gas mask in 1914. But nobody was interested in buying it. In July 1916 a tunnel collapsed in Cleveland, Ohio. Thirty workers were trapped 250 feet (76 m) below Lake Erie. Smoke and dust made it impossible for rescuers to reach the workers. Then someone remembered Morgan's mask. By using the mask, rescuers could breathe through the smoke and dust. The rescuers saved the workers. Orders for the mask rolled in from all over the country.

# PET WATERER

**1 PROBLEM** Your pet drinks so much that his water bowl is always empty. What kind of device would fill a water bowl automatically?

**2 PRINCIPLE** What happens when you suck water into a straw and then hold your finger over one end? The water stays in the straw until you remove your finger. When you remove your finger, air pressure pushes the water out. You can use this principle to make a pet waterer.

**3 IDEAS** Can you think of any ways to control how air enters the waterer? Doing so would allow water to come out when you want it to. You could place a **valve** on the waterer that lets air in when your pet's dish is empty. But can you come up with a way that your pet can control the valve?

**4 PLAN**
Gather together:
- ✔ large plastic jar with lid
- ✔ drill
- ✔ ⅜ inch drill bit
- ✔ water
- ✔ pie tin

valve—a movable part that controls the flow of liquid or gas

CREATE

**1** Put the lid on the jar and tighten it. Ask an adult to drill a hole through the side of the lid into the jar.

**2** Open the lid, and fill the jar with water. Replace the lid so that the holes in the lid and the jar line up perfectly.

**3** Carefully place the jar upside down inside the pie tin.

**4** Watch the tin fill with water. It stops filling when the water level covers the hole. It refills after your pet drinks enough to let more air in through the hole.

**6** IMPROVE

Does your pet waterer work? Does the tin refill each time your pet drinks? What other kinds of valves could you use?

# SNACK RAFT

**1 PROBLEM** It's a bother getting out of the pool to get something to drink. How could you stay afloat and quench your thirst at the same time?

**2 PRINCIPLE** The key to floating is **buoyancy**. Buoyancy means that if an object's **density** is less than water, it will float.

**3 IDEAS** Some materials that are less dense than water are foam or air. Can you use containers full of air to make a raft float?

**4 PLAN**

Gather together:
- ✔ ruler
- ✔ 12-inch (30-cm) x 18-inch (46-cm) piece of plywood
- ✔ pencil
- ✔ 2 empty 2-liter soda bottles with caps
- ✔ 4 14-inch (36-cm) long x ¾-inch (2-cm) wide strips of polyester elastic
- ✔ heavy duty staple gun

**buoyancy**—a natural phenomenon that occurs when an object is less dense than water and is pushed up by water pressure, making it float

**density**—how heavy or light an object is for its size

**1** Measure 5 inches (13 cm) in from one end of the plywood. Draw a vertical line at this point. Repeat this step on the other end of the plywood.

**2** Lay one of the bottles on its side along the line made in step 1.

**3** Lay one elastic strip across the bottle about one third of the way from its top. Use the stapler to staple one end of the elastic to the board beside the bottle.

**4** Stretch the elastic tightly over the bottle and staple the other side of the elastic to the board.

**5** Repeat steps 2 through 4 with another strip. This time lay the strip about one third of the way from the bottom of the bottle.

*CONTINUED ON NEXT PAGE* ➜

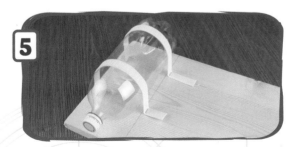

**6** Remove the bottle from the straps. Then repeat steps 2 through 5 with the other bottle at the second line.

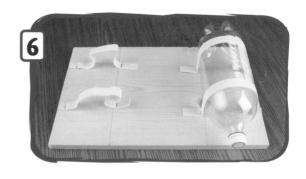

**7** Place both bottles in the straps and float the raft in a pool, tub, or lake.

**6 IMPROVE**

How much weight can your raft carry? Will more bottles make the raft more balanced? Think of other ways to make your raft float.

# EGG PARACHUTE

**1** **PROBLEM** Eggs crack with the slightest bump. What kind of contraption will protect an egg that is dropped from a large height?

**2** **PRINCIPLE** Look at the principles that NASA has used in landing some of its spacecraft. Astronauts slow down the craft by using parachutes to increase **air resistance**. And they land it in the ocean to softly cushion its landing. You need to find a way to make the egg fall slowly and land softly.

**3** **IDEAS** Balloons, propellers, and parachutes can increase air resistance. Bubble wrap, crumpled papers, or stuffing can cushion a landing. Try putting together a combination of these items to make the egg fall slowly and land softly.

**4** **PLAN**

Gather together:
- a small, square plastic container with a lid
- hole punch
- ruler
- scissors
- thread
- 4 plastic grocery bags
- poly-fill stuffing
- egg

**air resistance**—the drag that air puts on an object to slow it down

CONTINUED ON NEXT PAGE →

 **CREATE**

**1** Remove the lid from the container. Use the hole punch to make two holes in one corner of the container's lip.

**2** Measure and cut 24 inches (61 cm) of thread. Pull the thread down through one hole and up through the other. Pull the ends of the threads even.

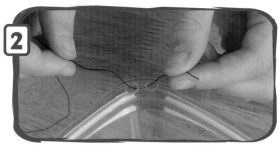

**3** Tie the ends of the thread around the handles of a grocery bag.

**4** Repeat steps 1 through 3 at each of the other three corners of the container.

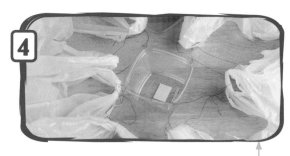

**5** Fill the container with poly-fill. Nest the egg in the center of the cotton. Place the lid back on the container.

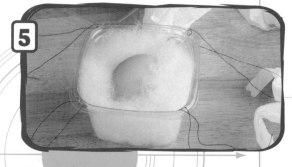

**6** Drop the container from a high location, such as a ladder or deck.

**IMPROVE**

Did the parachutes fill with air? Did your egg land without breaking? What other ideas can you use to make an egg fall slowly and land softly? Experiment with some other possibilities.

## ➡ DEVELOP YOUR SPECIAL SKILLS

In 1812, 3-year-old Louis Braille lost his eyesight in an accident. As he grew up, Louis learned a lot by listening. But he wanted to be able to read books. While attending a school for the blind, Louis learned how to read words by touching raised letters. But he thought there must be a better way for blind people to read. He started experimenting. He used needles to punch holes in paper. At age 15, he invented a way to represent letters, numbers, and symbols by using just six raised dots. The dots were arranged in different orders. Louis used his loss to benefit others. He invented a way for blind people to read.

# TOOTHPICK BRIDGE

**1 PROBLEM** Toothpicks are great for getting broccoli out of your teeth. But do they have other uses? Could they be used to build a bridge?

**2 PRINCIPLE** Arches are structures that do not need connections. The weight of their pieces holds them together. Stone arches stack stone **wedges** together. Each stone pushes on those next to it. The more weight you place on the arch, the tighter it holds together.

**3 IDEAS** Can you think of a shape you can make out of toothpicks that will allow you to wedge pieces together to make an arch?

**4 PLAN**

Gather together:
- ✔ toothpicks
- ✔ hot glue gun and glue

**wedge**—a piece of wood, rock, or metal that is thin at one end and thick at the other

**1** Arrange four toothpicks in a tic-tac-toe shape. Carefully hot glue the toothpicks in place. Make at least three more tic-tac-toe shapes. Allow them time to dry completely.

**2** Place two tic-tac-toe pieces side-by-side on a table. Slide the pieces together slightly. Allow the arms of one piece to slide inside the arms of the other.

**3** Place two toothpicks inside these overlapping arms.

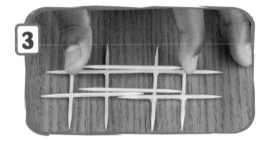

**4** Carefully arch the tic-tac-toe pieces upward. A tiny triangle will form between these pieces and the toothpicks from step 3.

**5** Thread a toothpick through these triangles. A small arch will form. Push on its center to see the arch tighten.

**6** Repeat steps 2 through 5 to make your bridge longer.

**6** IMPROVE

How big could you make your bridge? When you pressed on it, did it seem stronger? Try making a bridge from sticks, lumber, or other materials.

# GLOSSARY

**air resistance** (AIR ri-ZISS-tuhnss)—the force of air rubbing against things; air resistance slows down moving vehicles, such as cars and airplanes

**buoyancy** (BOI-yuhn-see)—a natural phenomenon that occurs when an object is less dense than water and is pushed up by water pressure, making it float

**classification** (klass-uh-fuh-KAY-shuh)—separating objects into groups by size, shape, or weight

**density** (DEN-si-tee)—how heavy or light an object is for its size

**force** (FORSS)—any action that changes the movement of an object

**galvanize** (GAL-vuh-nize)—to coat steel or iron with zinc to keep it from rusting

**hinge** (HINJ)—a movable joint

**patent** (PAT-uhnt )—a legal document giving an inventor sole rights to make and sell an item he or she invented

**pulley** (PUL-ee)—a grooved wheel turned by a rope, belt, or chain that often moves heavy objects

**truss** (TRUHSS)—a wooden or metal framework used to support walls or a roof

**valve** (VALV)—a movable part that controls the flow of liquid or gas

**wedge** (WEJ)—a piece of wood, rock, or metal that is thin at one end and thick at the other

# READ MORE

**Bell-Rehwoldt, Sheri.** *The Kids' Guide to Building Cool Stuff.* Kids' Guides. Mankato, Minn.: Capstone Press, 2009.

**Brasch, Nicolas.** *Amazing Built Structures.* The Technology Behind. Mankato, Minn.: Smart Apple Media, 2011.

**Enz, Tammy.** *Build Your Own Fort, Igloo, and Other Hangouts.* Build It Yourself. Mankato, Minn.: Capstone Press, 2011.

**Way, Steve and Gerry Bailey.** *Structures.* Simply Science. Pleasantville, N.Y.: Gareth Stevens Pub., 2009.

# INTERNET SITES

FactHound offers a safe, fun way to find Internet sites related to this book. All of the sites on FactHound have been researched by our staff.

Here's all you do:

Visit *www.facthound.com*

Type in this code: 9781429676359

Check out projects, games and lots more at
**www.capstonekids.com**

# INDEX

## ABOUT THE AUTHOR

Tammy Enz became a civil engineer because of her awe of the massive steel bridges that spanned the Mississippi River. She just had to figure out how they worked. Today, she still likes tinkering and figuring out how things work. When she isn't tinkering, she fixes up old houses and conducts experiments in her garden and kitchen. Most of all, she loves reading books about anything and everything and asking "why?"

7-12